Y0-CPC-871

ACTIVISM IN ACTION
A HISTORY™

THE FIGHT FOR WOMEN'S RIGHTS

MARCIA AMIDON LUSTED

New York

To all women, past, present, and future, who have fought hard for our rights and our opportunities. May we always persist.

Published in 2020 by The Rosen Publishing Group, Inc.
29 East 21st Street, New York, NY 10010

First Edition

Library of Congress Cataloging-in-Publication Data

Names: Lusted, Marcia Amidon, author.
Title: The fight for women's rights / Marcia Amidon Lusted.
Description: First edition. | New York, NY : Rosen Publishing, 2020. | Series: Activism in action : a history | Includes bibliographical references and index.
Identifiers: LCCN 2018017504| ISBN 9781508185536 (library bound) | ISBN 9781508185529 (pbk.)
Subjects: LCSH: Women's rights—History—Juvenile literature. | Feminism—History—Juvenile literature.
Classification: LCC HQ1236 .L87 2019 | DDC 305.4209—dc23
LC record available at https://lccn.loc.gov/2018017504

Manufactured in China

On the cover: Activists have long-advocated for women's rights by participating in public demonstrations, including the 1912 Suffrage parade in New York City (*top*) and the 2017 International Women's Strike in fifty countries (*bottom*).

CONTENTS

INTRODUCTION 4

CHAPTER ONE
IN THE BEGINNING 8

CHAPTER TWO
STRUGGLING FOR THE VOTE 19

CHAPTER THREE
WORLD WAR II:
THE HOME FRONT AND BEYOND 32

CHAPTER FOUR
THE SECOND WAVE 45

CHAPTER FIVE
OUR BODIES, OUR RIGHTS 57

CHAPTER SIX
WOMEN'S LIBERATION 68

CHAPTER SEVEN
"NEVERTHELESS, SHE PERSISTED" 80

TIMELINE 94
GLOSSARY 96
FOR MORE INFORMATION 98
FOR FURTHER READING 101
BIBLIOGRAPHY 103
INDEX 108

INTRODUCTION

For as long as society has existed, there has been a conflict about the role of men and women, and whether or not women and men should have equal footing. While history tells us that women have seemingly been resigned or even content with their prescribed roles as wives, mothers, and housekeepers, it is also a fact that, historically, women's voices, experiences, and opinions have rarely been written down or remembered. Women's history has some powerful role models, like Queen Elizabeth, who ruled England in the late 1500s, half-mythical figures, like Queen Boudica, who led British Celtic tribes against the Romans in 60 CE, and Cleopatra, who ruled the Egyptians until 30 CE. But there have not been enough actual voices for women's rights from real women who struggled and suffered and worked and demanded equality with men, because the work they did and the words they spoke were not valued.

Women did not make much progress in gaining their rights until they began to be heard. In 1792, English writer Mary Wollstonecraft wrote

Elizabeth I, who ruled England and Ireland from 1558 to 1603, is considered by many to be the greatest monarch in British history.

a pamphlet called "A Vindication of the Rights of Woman," arguing that it wasn't that women were inferior to men, but only that they weren't given enough education to compete with men. She suggested that women should be given equal access to education and schooling and that a nation's well-being depended on the essential contributions of women. Slowly, more women broke down barriers to make their voices heard, to become educated, and to gain ground in seeking women's rights.

The history of women's rights in the United States and all around the world is one of women standing up and telling their stories, and then standing up to the forces that would keep them from being equal citizens and partners. Women's stories are essential to the struggle for equal rights. As author Rebecca Solnit wrote in the *Guardian* newspaper in 2017:

> *Being unable to tell your story is a living death, and sometimes a literal one. If no one listens when you say your ex-husband is trying to kill you, if no one believes you when you say you are in pain, if no one hears you when you say help, if you don't dare say help, if you have been trained not to bother people by saying help. If you are considered to be out of line when you speak up in a meeting, are not admitted into an*

> *institution of power, are subject to irrelevant criticism whose subtext is that women should not be here or heard. Stories save your life. And stories are your life.*

The fight for women's rights is not over, and perhaps never will be. But listening to the voices of women who have brought us to this point, and tracing the path that the feminist movement has followed will help to continue the forward motion that will move today's girls along the path to becoming women with equal rights and an equal place in their societies, tomorrow.

CHAPTER ONE

IN THE BEGINNING

From the vantage point of the twenty-first century, it can be difficult to imagine a time when women had virtually no rights, and often their fathers or husbands made their decisions for them. However, women living during the early years of the United States, in Colonial America, were strictly confined to rigid gender roles, had very little freedom of choice, and no legal rights. Much of this was due to strong religious values, which taught that women were to be subservient to men. Their role was to maintain the household and raise children. The Christian Bible taught that women were inferior to their male counterparts, and more given to sin, so they were subservient first to their fathers and then to their husbands. Under Colonial laws, single women could not sue or be sued or enter into contracts. Women might be taught to read, enabling them to read the Bible, but otherwise many women were not educated.

This young Puritan woman was taught the skills to be a good housewife and to be subservient to her husband.

BEING POWERLESS

A married woman was legally powerless. Her husband controlled all of her property, even that which was hers before she got married, and he had complete legal control of their children. Divorce was not allowed. Women could not vote. They could not speak during church services or town meetings and had no voice in selecting ministers or in town affairs. The Puritan leader William Bradford wrote, according to Gail Collins' *America's Women: 400 Years of Dolls, Drudges, Helpmates, and Heroines*, "Touching our government, you are mistaken if you think we admit women … for they are excluded, as both reason and nature teacheth they should be."

Women might contribute to the family finances by raising chickens for eggs and making butter, or by creating textiles. But these would be sold by her husband and, most often, the money remained under his control. Of course, there were exceptions, occasionally a woman was forced by her husband's absence to take over some control of family businesses. She could do the work of a printer, storekeeper, or farmer, but she couldn't actually have that title. The few occupations that were open to women were running a

SHE VOTED

One Colonial woman did manage to vote. Lydia Chapin Taft of Uxbridge, Massachusetts, went to the local town meeting in 1756. Because her husband had recently died, just before an important town vote concerning the French and Indian War, she cast a vote in his place. Taft would vote in a total of three town meetings, in 1756, 1758, and 1765. From 1775 to 1807, the constitution of the state of New Jersey permitted anyone with property valued at fifty pounds or more to vote, including single women. Taft was allowed to vote as a widow, but married women were not included because their property was considered to be their husband's.

tavern or being innkeepers since these jobs were closely related to running a house. Midwives were women, but some Colonial women worked as doctors as well. A woman known as Mistress Allyn served as an army surgeon during King Philip's War and was paid twenty pounds in British money. Of course, her male counterparts made three times as much money to do the same job.

"BETTER THAN YOUR BLACK-COATES"

Despite the somewhat bleak legal status of women in Colonial America, some did manage to assert themselves. Anne Hutchinson moved to Massachusetts with her husband in 1634. She was skilled in the art of healing and experienced at midwifery. She would eventually have fifteen children of her own. She also began holding religious discussions in her own home, based on her unusual religious conviction that, unlike the views held by the Puritans of Massachusetts, who saw religion only in terms of sinning, religion should be joyful and involve a direct relationship with God. Before long, Hutchinson was attracting large crowds of listeners and was described by one of them as "Preach[ing] better Gospell than any of your black-coates that have been at the Ninneversity [university]." Her outspokenness and strong mind eventually brought her before the General Court, and she was banished to Rhode Island with her family.

REMEMBER THE LADIES

Other women found ways to influence politics in subtle ways. Abigail Adams was the wife of

John Adams, a Founding Father and eventually the second president of the United States. She made sure to let her husband know her mind. John Adams was a member of the Continental Congress, and his wife wrote to him in March 1776, urging him not to forget about the nation's women as they fought to separate from England. According to the Adams Family Papers: An Electronic Archive, she wrote:

Abigail Adams, future First Lady of the United States, urged her husband to "remember the ladies."

> *In the new Code of Laws which I suppose it will be necessary for you to make I desire you would Remember the Ladies, and be more generous and favourable to them than your ancestors. Do not put such unlimited power into the hands of the Husbands. Remember all Men would be tyrants if they could. If perticuliar care and attention is not*

paid to the Laidies we are determined to foment a Rebelion, and will not hold ourselves bound by any Laws in which we have no voice, or Representation.

FEMALE REVOLUTIONARY VOICES

Mercy Otis Warren was another woman who made her voice heard during the American Revolution, but in an even more public way than Abigail Adams. Warren was a published poet, as well as a political playwright and satirist, using humor to criticize politics. Even though women were expected to remain silent concerning politics, Warren communicated with some of the revolution's greatest thinkers and became known as the leading female intellectual of her time. Her plays criticized British policies and officers, and her 1805 book *History of the Rise, Progress and Termination of the American Revolution* was among the first nonfiction books published by a woman in America.

Judith Sargent Murray was another female writer of the Revolutionary era, writing essays and plays. She met George and Martha Washington and Benjamin Franklin. She was also a determined supporter of women's rights, writing essays about women's equality, access to education, and the right to control their earnings. Murray argued that the new country would need intelligent citizens, and since women were given the task of raising and educating patriotic sons, they, too, should be educated. Her essay "On the Equality of the Sexes" was published in 1791 and notes the following, according to the National Women's History Museum:

> *Yes, ye lordly, ye haughty sex, our souls are by nature equal to yours; the same breath of God animates, enlivens, and invigorates us; and that we are not fallen lower than yourselves, let those witness who have greatly towered above the various discouragements by which they have been so heavily oppressed; … I dare confidently believe, that from the commencement of time to the present day, there hath been as many females, as males, who, by the mere force of natural powers, have merited the crown of applause; who, thus unassisted, have seized the wreath of fame.*

Murray was able to support herself and her family through her writing, although she was sometimes forced to use a male pseudonym to hide the fact that she was a woman.

IT HAPPENED IN SALEM

An episode of US history that will never be forgotten significantly affected women. The Salem witch trials, which took place in Salem, Massa-

During the Salem witch trials, many innocent women were accused of witchcraft and forced to defend themselves in court.

chusetts, from February 1692 until May 1693, were a series of arrests, imprisonments, hearings, and executions all based on accusations of witchcraft. When it was over, twenty people had been executed, fourteen of whom were women. Five more had died in prison.

Women were accusers and the majority of the accused. Those most likely to be branded as possible witches by their peers either exhibited unusual behavior and appearance or might have bothered their neighbors at some time. Women were already seen as morally weaker than men, and women who were adept at healing and remedies were also suspected of witchcraft. Women without husbands to protect them were also vulnerable. As Gail Collins says in her book *America's Women*, "seventeenth-century New England was a place full of women with personalities that were stronger than the society around them," making their words and actions more suspicious to accusers of witchcraft.

THE CULT OF DOMESTICITY

With the dawn of the 1800s, American women were able to move away from the roles they held in Colonial society and into a position where they could participate more widely in the world. After the American Revolution, girls and women were routinely taught to read and write, and women became some of the biggest consumers of books and magazines. Teaching became a respectable career for women, as well as factory jobs in places like the textile mills of Lowell, Massachusetts. But a woman's true calling was still considered to be in the home, raising children and keeping the household running smoothly. Most women were still dependent on fathers and husbands for safety and support. It would take another war, one that split the United States itself, to bring women into even greater visibility in public life and make them work for more equality.

Between 1820 and the Civil War, more American families became middle class. They no longer had to produce everything they ate and wore, and men were the providers who worked at jobs while women stayed home. The family became viewed as the backbone of society, and a woman's place was at home, in the private sphere. "True womanhood" meant adhering to four cardinal virtues, or characteristics: piety, purity, domesticity, and submissiveness. This value system prized women remaining at home and away from employment and limited their influence in the wider world.

CHAPTER TWO

STRUGGLING FOR THE VOTE

In the decades before the Civil War, which began in 1861, women had been increasingly involved in reform movements, such as the temperance movement that campaigned against the use of alcoholic beverages and the abolitionist movement, dedicated to freeing the African American slaves. Women were working in the settlement house movement, trying to help immigrants and poor women, particularly in cities, to live better lives. There were also religious movements and societies dedicated to moral reform. And in all of these various movements and reforms, women were playing increasingly important roles.

"TRUE WOMANHOOD" CHALLENGED

Women were still struggling with the idea of true womanhood and the cult of domesticity. They were supposed to be happy with their roles as wives,

Harriet Beecher Stowe (*front and center*) wrote the novel *Uncle Tom's Cabin*, which dealt with slavery. Stowe was an abolitionist.

mothers, and keepers of the home. But as women found their voices and turned their energies to societal reform, they also found themselves trying to pass legislation and be heard by government officials. Women were disenfranchised: without the legal right to vote, and without that powerful connection to government and elections, their concern for social and moral issues went unheard. Although suffrage was becoming an issue before the Civil War, abolitionists like Wendell Phillips argued that by adding the issue of women's suffrage, it would jeopardize abolition and that this was "the Negro's hour." He explained, as noted in *The New Book of Knowledge*, "Mixing the movements ... would lose for the Negro far more than we should gain for the woman." Elizabeth Cady Stanton, who was one of the great leaders of the suffrage movement, responded to Phillips by saying, "Do you believe the African race is composed entirely of males?"

By 1869, the Fifteenth Amendment granted all citizens the right to vote, no matter their race, skin color, or position of service. All African American men could now vote, even if they had been enslaved. The right to vote would allow women a greater ability to achieve reforms through government action. Why not extend the same voting privilege to women? It was this question that shifted the suffrage movement into high gear.

COWS AND TAXES

In Glastonbury, Connecticut, in 1873, two elderly sisters refused to pay the taxes due on their farm. Their property had been reassessed at a higher rate, as were the properties of two widows in town, increasing their tax bills. Men with neighboring properties did not see an increase. Abby Smith spoke at the town meeting, saying:

> ***The motto of our government is "proclaim liberty to all the inhabitants of the land," and here, where liberty is so highly extolled and glorified by every man in it, one-half of the inhabitants are not put under her laws, but are ruled over by the other half, who can take all they possess.***

The tax collector seized seven of their cows to pay the back taxes. A newspaper published Abby Smith's speech and it spread around the country. The Smith sisters' cows became famous as well, and flowers made from the hair of their tails were sold with a ribbon declaring "Taxation without Representation."

VOICES FOR SUFFRAGE

Elizabeth Cady Stanton, Susan B. Anthony, and Lucy Stone were three of the leaders of the suffrage movement. Elizabeth Cady Stanton had received what was a good education for a girl at that time but was primarily busy being a wife and the mother of seven children. She became involved with suffrage through the abolition movement. Susan B. Anthony grew up in a family that was active in politics. She, too, came to suffrage through the abolition movement, but also through the temperance movement. After being denied the chance to speak at a temperance event because she was a woman, Anthony realized that women had to have the ability to vote if they were to be successful with reforms. Lucy Stone was the daughter of committed abolitionist parents. She was the first woman from Massachusetts to earn a bachelor's degree. She became an outspoken voice for both the antislavery and suffrage movements.

COMING TOGETHER

As a result of the injustices that women felt after the passing of the Fifteenth Amendment, as well as their inability to be heard in the fights for reform, women began to approach suffrage more directly. They began organizing women's rights groups, such as the National Woman Suffrage Association (NWSA), created by Stanton and Anthony, and the American Woman

Photographed above are the state presidents and officers of the National American Woman Suffrage Association in 1892.

Suffrage Association (AWSA), created by Lucy Stone. The main difference between these two groups was that the NWSA was for women only, while the AWSA allowed men to join. Lucy Stone had supported the Fifteenth Amendment, even though it did not include women. She said, as noted in *The New Book of Knowledge*, "There are two great oceans; in the one is the black man, and in the other is the woman ... I will be thankful in my soul if any body can get out of the terrible pit." The difference in viewpoints between Stanton and Anthony on one side and Stone on the other created the rift that led to the formation of these two separate suffrage groups.

On July 9, 1848, five women met at the home of Jane Hunt in Waterloo, New York. Together, Elizabeth Cady Stanton, Lucretia Mott, Martha Wright, Mary Ann M'Clintock, and Jane Hunt planned the first women's rights convention, which took place in Seneca Falls, New York, on July 19, 1848. Even though the convention had not been advertised, three hundred people attended. On that day, Stanton made her first public speech. Included was the following, as reported by the National Park Service:

> *We are assembled to protest against a form of government, existing without the consent of the governed—to declare our right to be free as man is free, to be represented in the government which we are taxed to support, to have such disgraceful laws as give man the power to chastise and imprison his wife, to take the wages which she earns, the property which she inherits, and, in case of separation, the children of her love; laws test against such unjust laws as these that we are assembled today, and to have*

them, if possible, forever erased from our statute-books, deeming them as a shame and a disgrace to a Christian republic in the nineteenth century.

Stanton also read a Declaration of Sentiments, which was based on the Declaration of Independence, intending to express a goal of giving women the same rights and freedoms that the original declaration had given to men. Only women were permitted to be present on the first day of the convention, but the general public, including men, were welcomed for the second day.

SOJOURNER TRUTH'S "AIN'T I A WOMAN?"

Born a slave, Sojourner Truth escaped to freedom. She later became an abolitionist and women's rights activist. In 1851, she attended the Women's Rights Convention in Akron, Ohio, and gave the famous speech "Ain't I a Woman?" Below is an excerpt from sojournertruthmemorial.org:

That man over there says that women need to be helped into carriages, and lifted over ditches, and to have the best place everywhere. Nobody ever helps me into

Sojourner Truth escaped from slavery to become a women's rights activist and abolitionist.

carriages, or over mud-puddles, or gives me any best place! And ain't I a woman? Look at me! Look at my arm! I have ploughed and planted, and gathered into barns, and no man could head me! And ain't I a woman? I could work as much and eat as much as a man—when I could get it—and bear the lash as well! And ain't I a woman? I have borne thirteen children, and seen most all sold off to slavery, and when I cried out with my mother's grief, none but Jesus heard me! And ain't I a woman?

NEW TACTICS

By 1890, the two suffrage organizations had overcome their differences and merged into one, the National American Woman Suffrage Association. Stanton became its first president. The NAWSA decided that instead of focusing on how women should be given the same rights as men, they would instead focus on what women could bring to politics and the country by being able to vote. They insisted that women should be given the right to vote because they differed from men and could draw upon the elements of domesticity and create a "moral commonwealth" through their purity and morality as women.

A WINNING PLAN

Slowly, women were making progress. Wyoming became the first state to give women the right to vote in all elections in 1890. By 1910, other western states, including Idaho and Utah, followed suit. In 1916, the NAWSA president Carrie Chapman Catt launched what she called a "Winning Plan." It was a focused blitz campaign, using state and local groups, to work for suffrage. At the same time, the National Women's Party (NWP) used more radical tactics, such as picketing the White House and going on hunger strikes.

The advent of World War I, which the United States entered in 1917, slowed the suffrage movement. But women served as nurses overseas and at home. They also worked in factories that made weapons and munitions, doing the work that men had left behind when they went to war. Just before the war ended in 1918, President Woodrow Wilson encouraged Congress to pass an amendment in favor of women's suffrage. He said, "We have made partners of the women in this war. Shall we admit them only to a partnership of suffering and sacrifice and toil and not to a partnership of privilege and right?"

However, it was another year before the issue of women's suffrage was finally settled. On May

21, 1919, the US House of Representatives passed the Nineteenth Amendment, which made it possible for US citizens to vote regardless of one's gender. The Senate approved it on June 4, and by August 26, 1920, the necessary number of states had ratified the amendment. Women had finally been guaranteed the right to vote.

A NEW ERA

Women had the right to vote, and times were changing. The 1920s brought a new era of free-dom for women. The modern young woman,

During the 1920s, young women called flappers found new freedom in short skirts, bobbed hair, and jazz music.

especially the famous flapper of the 1920s, wore short dresses and makeup, got rid of corsets and long skirts, and cut her hair into a short bob. She was no longer bound by the morality of older generations. She was drinking and smoking, listening to jazz and going to parties, and exploring more sexual freedom. But the new freedom that flappers and other women in the twenties enjoyed was only a taste of what women wanted. They were still struggling with issues surrounding jobs, education, and homemaking. Another world war would bring these issues into sharper focus.

CHAPTER THREE

WORLD WAR II: THE HOME FRONT AND BEYOND

On December 7, 1941, the Japanese forces bombed Pearl Harbor, Hawaii. This unexpected attack catapulted the United States into World War II. They joined forces with Australia, Britain, Canada, China, France, India, New Zealand, and the Soviet Union as the Allied forces or the Allies. The Allies were fighting against the Axis powers of Germany, Japan, and Italy. The war would last until 1945 and take the lives of 416,800 American soldiers.

ON THE HOME FRONT

Almost from the start, American women had important roles to play during World War II. At first, the focus was on US households and how they could support the soldiers overseas by limiting their use of commodities such as gasoline, rubber, sugar, and meat. These kinds of commodities were in short supply because they were needed for war equipment or to feed soldiers overseas. Items like

On December 7, 1941, Japanese forces bombed the US naval base at Pearl Harbor, Hawaii, bringing the United States into World War II.

coffee and sugar, which were imported, were also limited due to wartime limits on imported goods. Items like these were rationed, meaning that each family was allowed only a certain amount. Everyone was issued a ration book, with removable stamps that had to be provided along with money when these goods were purchased. If a family ran out of stamps, they couldn't purchase any more of that item for the month. Women had to become very creative when it came to cooking meals for their families with limited foods.

Women were also responsible for growing victory gardens. These were vegetable gardens intended to supply families with fresh produce. Eventually, 60 percent of the produce that Americans ate was grown in their own victory gardens.

FIRST LADY ELEANOR ROOSEVELT

As wife of President Franklin D. Roosevelt, Eleanor Roosevelt was the longest-serving First Lady in US history. She served from 1933 until 1945 but was more noteworthy for the way in which she changed the role of First Lady. Instead of staying in the background and putting her energies into the domestic side of the White House, she gave press conferences, spoke in support of human rights issues, and wrote a newspaper column called "My Day." She particularly supported women's and children's issues. During World War II, Roosevelt toured the country to help open Civil Defense offices, wrote about war topics in her column, and even visited England, which was being bombed by Germans on a regular basis.

She visited hospitals and military and naval bases, as well as the Pacific Theater of the war. Roosevelt wrote in her column, of these visits to combat zones, "if the generation that fights today is to lay the foundations of which a peaceful world can be built, all of us who have seen the war close range must remember what we see and carry a crusading spirit into all of our work."

Eleanor Roosevelt was the longest-serving First Lady in US history and was especially supportive of women's and children's issues.

"A LARGE HORIZON" WITH FRANCES PERKINS

Eleanor Roosevelt was not the only woman to break through traditional barriers during World War II. In 1933, President Franklin Roosevelt's secretary of labor, Frances Perkins, became the first woman to hold a cabinet position. She was responsible for much of what would become the New Deal, programs designed to help the US economy during the Great Depression of the 1930s. She also helped draft the 1938 Fair Labor Act, which guaranteed a minimum wage and maximum work hours, and outlawed child labor. Perkins was one of only two cabinet secretaries to serve for the entire time that Roosevelt was president. After Roosevelt's death, she continued in government roles and then as a university professor. In a 1960 speech to the students of Syracuse University, Perkins said, "There is always a large horizon ... There is much to be done ... I am not going to be doing it! It is up to you to contribute some small part to a program of human betterment for all time."

EDUCATOR AND LEADER: MARY MCLEOD BETHUNE

Another remarkable woman of the Roosevelt era was Mary McLeod Bethune, who was an important black educator. She was a leader in the civil rights and women's rights movements, an advisor to President Roosevelt, and a close friend to Eleanor Roosevelt. Bethune was born in 1875 in South Carolina and grew up picking cotton on her family's farm. In 1936, she became the highest-ranking African American woman working in government.

It was then when Roosevelt named Bethune director of Negro affairs of the National Youth Administration. Bethune was also the president's advisor on matters concerning African Americans and worked to end discrimination and the practice of lynching. She later became vice president of the National Association for the Advancement of Colored People (NAACP). She was appointed by President Harry S. Truman as the only African American woman to attend the founding conference of the United Nations in 1945.

FROM HOMEMAKER TO FACTORY WORKER

The most important role that women played during World War II had nothing to do with homemaking, cooking, and growing vegetables. Because so many men had gone overseas as soldiers and sailors, they left behind a shortage of workers. For the first time, women were encouraged to take jobs outside of the home. They worked in defense plants, manufacturing munitions and equipment as well as ships and aircraft, or ran family businesses that their husbands had to leave behind. They also took clerical and office jobs. According to the National World War II Museum:

During World War II, many women found work in munitions factories, playing a vital role in the war effort.

> *[Women] drove trucks, repaired airplanes, worked as laboratory technicians, rigged parachutes, served as radio operators, analyzed photographs, flew military aircraft across the country, test-flew newly repaired planes, and even trained anti-aircraft artillery gunners by acting as flying targets.*

Others worked for organizations such as the Red Cross. While women could not serve in military conflict zones, auxiliary branches were created for every branch of the military. These included the Women's Army Corps (WAC), Women Accepted for Volunteer Emergency Service (WAVES), and Women Airforce Service Pilots (WASP). Other women served as nurses either in the United States or abroad, nursing men who had been injured in combat. In total, six million women worked in the defense industry, three million volunteered for the Red Cross, and more than two hundred thousand joined the military.

PUTTING WOMEN TO WORK

During World War II, American women were a valued and needed part of the war effort, especially in filling vacancies in factories and businesses. However, the Axis powers were very slow in bringing the women of their countries into their war effort. Adolf Hitler, head of the Nazi Party, criticized the United States for putting its women to work. Hitler declared that the only role for women was that of being a good wife and to birth more babies for the Third Reich, another name for Nazi-controlled Germany. Women who had four or more children were even awarded a medal known as the Motherhood Cross.

The war gave women the opportunity to gain freedom and independence that they had never before experienced. Between 1940 and 1945, the number of women working outside the home rose from 27 percent to 37 percent, and by 1945 nearly one out of every four married women were employed. They were free to work in industries that were previously limited to men, such as being steelworkers, streetcar conductors, and airplane pilots. Many women enjoyed entering the working world so much that they hoped to retain their jobs

WE CAN DO IT!

One of the most iconic posters of World War II featured a strong young woman, wearing a bandana over her hair. A speech bubble above her head reads, "We can do it!" This propaganda poster, created by the US government, was part of a campaign to get more women into the workforce, especially in industries such as aviation, which weren't traditionally female occupations. The woman in the poster was nicknamed Rosie the Riveter since riveting was an important part of the process for building airplanes. There was even a popular 1943 song called "Rosie the Riveter," with lyrics that stated:

All the day long whether rain or shine
She's a part of the assembly line
She's making history,
working for victory
Rosie the Riveter
Keeps a sharp lookout for sabotage
Sitting up there on the fuselage
That little frail can do more than a male
will do
Rosie the Riveter.

This iconic poster of Rosie the Riveter promotes the strength and willingness of women who filled jobs left vacant by men who went off to war.

even when the war was over. However, when the fighting ended, not only did the demand for war materials decrease, requiring fewer factory workers, but also the men returning home from the war needed employment and reclaimed jobs that were being done by women. The brief, exhilarating days of more equality in the workplace ended almost as quickly as they had begun.

THE 1950S AND SUBURBIA

Even though women were replaced in the working world by returning World War II veterans, not all women were unhappy about returning to their previous roles. With the return of American men from the war, suddenly marriage, housekeeping, and childbearing became the ideal female roles once more. This social role was reinforced by the media and advertising, and since women did most of the buying for their households, advertisers began aiming ads and product designs at women. Magazines showed women as homemakers and mothers, who were happy simply because their families were taken care of and some of their household chores had been made easier by new technologies. And yet not every 1950s woman was happy in a domestic role. Even with the loss of war jobs, women were entering the workplace in greater numbers. By 1956, 35 percent of all adult women were working outside of the home. The divorce rate increased as well, and by the end of the decade, one in every 3.8 marriages ended in divorce. Some of this was due to a prosperous economy since women who felt they could support themselves were more likely to get divorced.

One of the voices of this era belonged to French writer and philosopher Simone de Beauvoir. Her

Simone de Beauvoir's book *The Second Sex*, published in 1953, was one of the first important works of feminism.

book *The Second Sex*, published in the United States in 1953, discussed the second-rate status that women had endured throughout history, and talked of a society where men held most of the power and women had very little. The book is one of the first and most important works of feminism and established de Beauvoir as a feminist icon. However, its discussion of female anatomy and of lesbian relationships made it extremely controversial.

PAVING THE WAY

De Beauvoir's book, as well as the growing discontent of women with the roles that had been foisted upon them during the 1950s and an increasing ability to work outside the home, were paving the way for a more concentrated feminist movement. As the decade ended and the 1960s dawned with the civil rights movement and Vietnam War, women started demanding more than ever before an equal place for themselves.

CHAPTER FOUR

THE SECOND WAVE

The 1960s were a time of unrest. The Vietnam War was being fought by American soldiers, and many Americans protested the United States' involvement in this war. Many were also marching in protest as part of the civil rights movement, wanting to gain equal rights and end segregation for African Americans. Times were also changing for women. The "ideal" domestic role for women as homemakers, wives, and mothers was constricting, and many began actively seeking equal rights for themselves.

THE TIME HAS COME

One of the signs that the women's rights movement was gaining visibility was the formation of the President's Commission on the Status of Women. On December 14, 1961, it was established by executive order of President John F. Kennedy. The role of the commission was to

Civil rights protesters gathered in Montgomery, Alabama, on March 29, 1965, after their march from Selma to protest voter registration laws in the state.

evaluate and then make recommendations to improve the economic, legal, social, and civic status of women in America. Initially the commission was chaired by Eleanor Roosevelt, a position she held until her death in 1962. Executive Vice Chairman Esther Peterson, assistant secretary of labor and director of the US Women's Bureau, served after Roosevelt. The commission released a report on October 11, 1963. Among its recommendations were to end sexual discrimination in hiring for jobs, to implement paid maternity leave and universal child care, and to acquire the legal recognition of women's status under the Fourteenth Amendment to the Constitution, which in 1866 granted citizenship to all people born in the United States.

Women were seeking equal rights but also, more importantly, an equal voice. Many were discontented with the roles they had been forced into during the 1950s. One emerging voice for women was Betty Friedan, who had graduated from Smith College in 1942. She worked as a reporter in New York City and then married in 1947. She continued to work after having her first child but lost her job when she became pregnant with her second child. Friedan then became a homemaker but found herself restless and bored in the role. She wondered if other women from her college felt the same way and sent a survey to other graduates of Smith College. The feedback Friedan received became the basis for her book, *The Feminine Mystique*, published in 1963. The book dispelled the myth that all women desired to become homemakers and revealed that many of them were unhappy as housewives. It challenged the assumption that "fulfillment as a woman had only one definition for American women after 1949—the

Betty Friedan wrote *The Feminine Mystique* and also helped to found the National Organization for Women, known as NOW.

housewife-mother." Friedan also researched psychology, media, and advertising as it reinforced this message to women. She ended the book with examples of real women who had fought against stereotypical roles and encouraged all women to seek new opportunities in their lives. *The Feminine Mystique* became the bestselling nonfiction book of 1964, proving that Friedan's message struck a nerve with many American women.

Friedan had become one of the strongest voices for women's rights in the 1960s, and she would go on to found, with others, an important organization working for the rights of women. The following notes from ObamaWhiteHouse.archives.gov state:

> *On June 30, 1966, Betty Friedan wrote three letters on a paper napkin: N O W. She invited fifteen women to her hotel room. Then, Catherine Conroy slid a five-dollar bill onto the table and said, "Put your money down and sign your name." In that moment, the National Organization for Women became a reality.*

The women who founded NOW wanted to put an end to sex discrimination, and the organization has been a cornerstone for women's rights. According to its statement of purpose:

We, men and women who hereby constitute ourselves as the National Organization for Women, believe that the time has come for a new movement toward true equality for all women in America, and toward a fully equal partnership of the sexes, as part of the world-wide revolution of human rights now taking place within and beyond our national borders.

Friedan was chosen as NOW's first president at its initial conference in October 1966. Some of the first activities that NOW participated in were picketing the *New York Times* in August 1967 to protest help-wanted ads that were segregated by gender; Take Back the Night marches and vigils in 1973 to protest sexual assault and personal violence against women; and the March for Women's Lives in Washington, DC, in April 2004, when 1.15 million people marched for women's reproductive rights and health care options.

MAKING AN IMPACT

Another founding member of NOW was Reverend Addie L. Wyatt. In addition to working for

Reverend Addie Wyatt is shown here speaking at the first Coalition of Labor Union Women convention in Chicago in 1974. She helped found NOW and also worked in the civil rights movement.

women's rights, she was also involved in the civil rights movement and was one of the United States's foremost labor union leaders. She was the first woman to spearhead a local labor union and the first to become an international vice president of the Amalgamated Meat Cutters and Butcher Workmen of North America union. From

1956 until 1968, Wyatt teamed up with Reverend Martin Luther King Jr. in several major civil rights marches. She also became director of the Women's Affairs and Human Rights departments in the Amalgamated Meat Cutters. Because of Wyatt's successful leadership, Eleanor Roosevelt asked her to be a part of the Labor Legislation Committee of the Commission on the Status of Women in the early 1960s. She was also one of the founders of the Coalition of Labor Union Women (CLUW) in 1974. The following year, Wyatt became one of *Time* magazine's women of the year.

THE CIVIL RIGHTS ACT OF 1964

A piece of landmark legislation for both the civil rights movement and the women's movement was the Civil Rights Act of 1964. It was intended to stop discrimination in the application of voter registration laws, as well as end segregation in schools, workplaces, and public facilities. Title VII of the act gave women hope, as it prohibits employment discrimination based on one's color, race, religion, national origin, and sex.

BECOME ITS SOUL

Coretta Scott King was one of the most influential women of her time. As the wife of Martin Luther King Jr., she worked with him closely in the civil rights movement and continued the work after his assassination in 1968. But she was also an advocate for women's and children's rights, racial and economic justice, environmental justice, and democracy, as well as many other issues. She once said the following about women's role in society: "Women, if the soul of the nation is to be saved, I believe that you must become its soul." In 1968, King also founded the Martin Luther King Jr. Center for Nonviolent Social Change in memory of her husband. She became one of the most influential female leaders in the world.

Coretta Scott King and her husband, Reverend Martin Luther King Jr., participate in a march to the state capitol in Montgomery, Alabama, in 1965.

STEPPING UP TO SERVE

Martha Griffiths was a member of the US House of Representatives from 1955 until 1974, as a Democrat from Michigan. She was the first woman to serve on the House Ways and Means Committee, a powerful committee responsible for creating taxes, as well as overseeing tariffs, trade agreements, and bonded debt. Griffiths played a key role in getting discrimination based on gender included in the 1964 Civil Rights Act. In 1970, she resurrected the Equal Rights Amendment (ERA), which was first drafted by suffragist Alice Paul in 1923.

However, when it came to enforcing the portion of the act that related to women, very little was done. Often the act was treated as a joke among men. Because federal officials in charge of enforcement were treating women's issues with contempt, it became clear that only outside pressure on the government would create any actual change concerning discrimination based on gender. NOW was one organization that was created to do this, but its campaigns in favor of abortion and the Equal Rights Amendment alienated many of its more conservative members. As a result, Elizabeth Boyer, an Ohio lawyer and founding member of NOW, created the Women's Equity Action League (WEAL). WEAL, according to WorldHistory.biz, "avoided issues 'that polarize people—like The [birth control] Pill, or issue and instead focused on legal and employment issues that affected women, as well as women's health care in general. WEAL's tactics were also different from NOW in that they encouraged "feminine" behavior, made "requests" instead of demands, and looked for reforms and compromises. Although WEAL became more aggressive in later years, the organization was dissolved in 1989.

GOT KIDS? NO JOB FOR YOU

In 1971, the Supreme Court settled its first discrimination case based on Title VII of the Civil Rights Act of 1964. Ida Phillips sued Martin Marietta, a supplier of heavy building materials. The company refused to hire her because of a policy that job applications would not be accepted from women who had preschool-age children. The assumption was that women with young children might have to call in sick more frequently in order to stay home and care for their young children. The Supreme Court ruled in Phillips's favor because Martin Marietta's policy of not hiring workers with preschool-aged children did not apply to men and therefore showed a bias.

A DECADE OF CHANGE

While much of the work for women's rights continued into the 1970s and the present day, the 1960s were a decade that saw many gains for women. Americans became familiar with and even accepting of some of the basic goals of feminists: that they should receive equal pay for equal work, have equal access to jobs on the management level, not be sexually harassed, and that men should share the responsibilities for housekeeping and child care. It also became more common to see women in roles that had traditionally belonged to men, such as broadcasting, diplomatic roles, and justices of the Supreme Court.

One of the biggest issues for feminists, as well as being an area where traditional morals and perspectives changed drastically, was in health care. Women's health, including their rights to control their reproductive health and the need for health care practitioners and facilities dedicated to women's health, has involved controversial issues then and continues to today.

CHAPTER FIVE

OUR BODIES, OUR RIGHTS

One of biggest issues that women faced following World War II was the question of their own health, particularly when it came to their reproductive health. Women were no longer satisfied to occupy the role of "ideal woman," as mothers whose purpose was to have as many children as possible. Women were making professional gains, with jobs and careers outside of the home. This often resulted in many women wanting to limit the size of their families.

"CAN THEY NOT USE SELF CONTROL?"

For much of US history, women had very little choice about pregnancy. With few reliable birth control options, many endured pregnancy after pregnancy, often leading to illness or death. "Nice" women didn't use birth control, or at least they did not admit to it. The question of contraception for women became even more controversial

Women fought for the right to access safe, effective forms of birth control as well as accurate information about women's health issues.

because of a law passed by Congress in 1873 that prohibited the dissemination through the postal service "of obscene literature and articles of immoral use," this included any birth control literature, devices, or drugs. This law, which became known as the Comstock Laws, as it became a series of acts, had been pushed by Anthony Comstock, a lobbyist and crusader who spent much of his life confiscating what he felt was obscene material and arresting thousands of people who did not obey the law. When asked whether it was acceptable for a woman to use contraception if her life would be endangered by a pregnancy, he told the journalist, as quoted in *America's Women: 400 Years of Dolls, Drudges, Helpmates, and Heroines*, "Can they not use self control? Or must they sink to the level of the beasts?" The greatest consequence of the Comstock Laws was that before 1915, contraception was difficult to find and not talked about.

OPENING THE DOORS

The woman who helped bring birth control to the public's eye, and who crusaded for women to have the right to limit the size of their families, was Margaret Sanger. She was one of eleven children in her family and once stated that her mother's death at age fifty was from "having too many children and working herself to death." Sanger married and had three children when family finances made it necessary for her to get a job. That led her to working for the visiting nurse association on New York City's Lower East Side. Sanger began to see many women whose lives were being ruined by too many pregnancies and who were using home remedies like turpentine or knitting needles to induce abortions. These women often died from septicemia, or blood poisoning. As a result, Sanger led a crusade

Margaret Sanger (*left*), advocate for birth control, smiles after her coworkers are found not guilty in a Harlem court of charges of distributing birth control information.

to educate women about birth control, first using a self-published newspaper and then by giving lectures. This brought her into contact with Comstock, who arrested her eight times, causing Sanger and contraception to become a household name and concept.

"WHAT EVERY GIRL SHOULD KNOW"

One of Sanger's first efforts to make contraceptive information available was a column that she wrote for *The Call*, a daily socialist newspaper. Her column was called "What Every Girl Should Know" and covered many areas of sex education. However, Sanger's article about venereal disease was banned by Comstock. On that day, *The Call* ran an empty space with the title, "What Every Girl Should Know. Nothing; by order of the U.S. Post Office."

By the 1920s, Sanger had helped to defeat the Comstock Laws legislation and brought women's reproductive health to the medical and scientific community. She eventually helped open a network of birth control clinics (the predecessors of today's Planned Parenthood), where women could access the most reliable forms of contraception available at the time and receive real information about reproductive health.

BROADER TERMS WITH EMMA GOLDMAN

One pioneer in the world of women and on the subject of birth control was Emma Goldman, who served as a mentor to Margaret Sanger. The Russian-born Goldman, who later became an anarchist and writer, came to the United States at age sixteen. Goldman introduced Sanger to the freedom of speech movement against the Comstock Laws and urged her to become involved. Goldman believed that birth control was directly related to the issues of sexual and economic freedom for women. She insisted that reproductive rights and the suppression of birth control had to be viewed in the broader terms of political, social, and economic rights for women.

THE PILL

Because of women like Sanger, who were willing to bring the issue of birth control and reproductive rights into the public light, the federal ban on birth control was lifted by 1938. However, the use of contraceptives was still technically illegal. In 1965, the Supreme Court case *Griswold v. Connecticut* ruled that the use of birth control was legal for married couples but still illegal for single women. In 1951, Sanger met an endocrinologist named Gregory Pincus. She persuaded him to begin working on the development of a birth control pill. Sanger also helped find funding for the research, and after testing, a birth control pill was approved by the Food and Drug Administration (FDA) in 1957. However, it was approved only for use in helping women with severe menstrual period disorders. Of course, after the FDA approval, an unusually large number of women began reporting that they had menstrual disorders. Finally, in 1960, the Pill was approved for contraceptive use. It was immediately popular. By 1962, 1.2 million women were taking the Pill, and by the following year, the number jumped to 2.3 million. However, controversy continued regarding the Pill because of religious objections and because early versions of

Gregory Pincus developed the birth control pill, approved as a contraceptive in 1960.

the Pill caused serious side effects. Newer formulations of the Pill have minimized the early health risks, and in 1972, the Supreme Court case *Baird v. Eisenstadt* legalized birth control for all American citizens, regardless of their marital status.

The Pill, as well as other methods of contraception that have been developed, gave women the right to control when and if they wanted to have children. Along with this choice, some women began to change how they perceived pregnancy and childbirth.

A NATURAL BIRTH

For much of the country's history, women gave birth at home, attended by a friend, midwife, or family doctor. The twentieth century brought a shift: babies were born in hospitals, medical staff was in attendance, and more medications were used to control the pain of contractions. This coincided with a belief that doctors were the most qualified professionals to attend deliveries. Hospital births were considered to be safer, and more families were able to afford the cost. During the 1950s and 1960s in the United States, most women gave birth under heavy anesthesia, a medicine meant to minimize pain. This put women into a kind of "twilight sleep," in which they were barely aware of the birth and were groggy for the first moments of their babies' lives. However, many women became concerned about the effects of anesthesia on the baby and wanted to be awake for the birthing experience or care for their newborns immediately. Local anesthesia was then developed for use during childbirth, such as spinal anesthesia, which relieved pain without putting the patient to sleep. However, sometimes mothers were still unable to push during delivery, and those babies were often delivered using forceps.

OUR BODIES, OURSELVES

In May 1969, twelve women met during a women's liberation conference in Boston, Massachusetts. They attended a workshop called "Women and Their Bodies" and discussed their own experiences with doctors and the medical system. As a result of their meeting, they established the Boston Women's Health Collective, to research and discuss issues of women's health. Eventually they published a book called *Our Bodies, Ourselves* (and later renamed their group to share the same name). The book included frank discussions of sexuality and abortion and urged women to take ownership of their own health. The book has been routinely updated every four to six years since its initial printing.

The natural childbirth movement supported the choices of birthing women, particularly the ability to choose to give birth in a nonhospital setting and with minimal medical intervention.

As the feminist movement strengthened, so did the push to involve women in their own labor and deliveries. The push became known as the natural childbirth movement. Pioneers of the movement included researchers who created new systems for childbirth, such as Lamaze, which focused on pain relief and control through breathing patterns, relaxation, hypnosis, and giving birth while immersed in water. These new systems offered more relaxed environments, including the patients' homes, and offered more choice in the kind of childbirth experience they wanted to have and whom they wanted to give them care (midwives or doctors). The systems also pushed for a shift in doctor/patient relationships, with greater agency for the patient and allowing for more choice in consenting to a procedure.

Women were slowly gaining control when it came to their reproductive health. More and more, they began planning their pregnancies and deciding how they wanted to bring their babies into the world. But the larger issue of women's rights was still a divisive and much-discussed topic across the nation.

CHAPTER SIX

WOMEN'S LIBERATION

Women were struggling to gain equal rights with men and to be seen as something other than wives, mothers, and housekeepers. As one woman put it, "I'm desperate. I begin to feel I have no personality. I'm a server of food and a putter-on of pants and a bedmaker, somebody who can be called on when you want something. But who am I?" Woman had begun to assert their power in reproductive health and family planning, but they wanted more. After the publication of Simone de Beauvoir's *The Second Sex* and Betty Freidan's *The Feminine Mystique*, the second wave of feminism had taken shape. Women were ready to continue the fight begun by those who fought for suffrage. This new iteration of the feminist movement was dubbed women's liberation because women were seeking freedom from the roles they had previously been controlled and limited by.

FROM MRS. TO *MS.*

One of the media voices that helped the feminist movement gain momentum was *Ms.* magazine,

The women's liberation movement brought many women into the streets to protest and demand equal rights.

a publication started by Gloria Steinem in 1972. *Ms.* got its start as a test insert in *New York* magazine in December 1971. In 1972, it hit national newsstands as its own publication, and in as few as eight days, the three hundred thousand test copies had sold out! Despite network news anchor Harry Reasoner's comment, "I'll give it six months before they run out of things to say," *Ms.* had twenty-six thousand subscribers and received twenty thousand letters in just weeks. It was an independent voice for women who wanted to read about something other than cooking, housekeeping, cosmetics, and child rearing. *Ms.* soon moved from being something for people to ridicule to showing that feminism was something to be taken seriously. As the magazine itself says on its About page:

> Ms. *was the first US magazine to feature prominent American women demanding the repeal of laws that criminalized abortion, the first to explain and advocate for the ERA, to rate presidential candidates on women's issues, to put domestic violence and sexual harassment on the cover of a women's magazine, to feature feminist protest of pornography, to commission and feature a national study on date rape, and to blow the whistle on the undue influence of advertising on magazine journalism.* Ms. *was the first national magazine to make feminist voices audible, feminist journalism tenable, and a feminist worldview available to the public.*

THE ERA

During the suffrage movement, before women had the right to vote, activist Alice Paul believed that only an amendment to the US Constitution would ensure that women would be free from legalized discrimination based on their sex. She introduced a 1923 amendment called the Lucretia Mott Amendment, which stated: "Men and women shall have equal rights throughout the United States and every place subject to its jurisdiction." The language of the amendment shifted over time to become the Equal Rights Amendment (ERA), which reads:

> *Section 1. Equality of rights under the law shall not be denied or abridged by the United States or by any state on account of sex.*
> *Section 2. The Congress shall have the power to enforce, by appropriate legislation, the provisions of this article.*
> *Section 3. This amendment shall take effect two years after the date of ratification.*

The ERA passed in the US Senate and the House of Representatives on March 22, 1972, as the proposed Twenty-Seventh Amendment to the Constitution. However, proposed amendments must be ratified by three-fourths of the states (a total of thirty-eight out of fifty), and within seven years. By 1979, only thirty-five states had ratified the ERA. NOW organized a march of one hundred thousand supporters in Washington, DC, in 1978. As a result, Congress approved an extension until June 30, 1982.

Alice Paul introduced the Lucretia Mott Amendment in 1923, the forerunner of the Equal Rights Amendment.

But even with the extra time, the ERA was not ratified by enough states. It has been continually reintroduced to Congress but has yet to pass. However, as Alice Paul said of the amendment she introduced in 1923, which still applies to the ERA, "We shall not be

STOP ERA!

Not every woman active in politics automatically supported the passage of the ERA. Phyllis Schlafly, a conservative author, activist, and lawyer, as well as an advocate for stay-at-home wives and mothers, is often said to have single-handedly prevented the passage of the ERA in the 1970s, helping the Republican Party and conservatives move to a focus on family and religion. Schlafly opposed the ERA based on a belief that it would lead to abortions, coed bathrooms, and same-sex marriages, as well as the military draft for women and the end of labor laws barring women from work environments that were considered dangerous. She started a national organization called Stop ERA, which later became known as the Eagle Forum. Schlafly called the organization an alternative to women's liberation.

safe until the principle of equal rights is written into the framework of our government."

FIGHTING FOR FAIRNESS

Despite the frustration over being unable to gain enough state support for the ERA, women were still fighting for equal opportunities, equal pay, and the ability to hold any job that a man could hold. Women had struggled to access a college education, but then once it became acceptable for them to participate in higher education, they still struggled to find positions in colleges and universities as professors and administrators. Since 1979, women have earned more than half of all bachelor's and master's degrees awarded by American universities and one-third of all doctorate degrees. But even as late as 2012, 86 percent of all high-level administrative positions in universities, such as presidents and chancellors, were held by men, and 75 percent of all full professors were male. Female professors are still likely to have lower salaries and higher teaching loads than men and are slower to advance in their careers. This gender gap in position and salary, across a wide range of industries, continues today.

The 1970s, however, saw the creation of many women's studies programs at colleges and universities. It was a time when just to say that women should be studied as a serious academic field was radical, but many feminists felt that academic acknowledgement was just as important to women's rights as political activism. Women's studies was directly related to creating social change. At first, many women's studies classes could not even access funding for professors and materials and were often held for free, and in private homes. Women also had to fight against a prevailing conservative opinion that education was about studying white men and that women who enrolled in women's studies courses or majors

The women's rights movement made college courses in gender and women's studies an accepted part of the university curriculum.

were a threat. Pat Robertson, a conservative Christian politician and former minister, is quoted by InsideHigherEd.com as saying the following with regards to women's studies: "The feminist agenda is not about equal rights for women. It is about a socialist, anti-family political movement that encourages women to leave their husbands, kill their children, practice witchcraft, destroy capitalism, and become lesbians." Despite reactions like these, women's studies has flourished, with more than eight hundred programs available in the United States, including PhD-level degree programs. Alice E. Ginsburg, an education consultant, notes the following on InsideHigherEd.com: "The whole idea of women's studies is to make visible what has been invisible and to make conscious what has been overlooked or silenced."

PAT SCHROEDER TAKES A LEAD

Pat Schroeder was the first woman to be elected to the US House of Representatives from the state of Colorado, with her term of service spanning from 1973 until 1997. At the time of her election, she was the mother of a six- and a two-year-old and wanted to demonstrate that women could be mothers and still work. At first, Schroeder's political rivals and male colleagues referred to her as Little Patsy, but she became a strong voice for important topics, such as women's reproductive rights and the arms race. She became a member of the Armed Services Committee, saying that "When men talk about defense, they always claim to be protecting women and children, but they never ask the women and children what they think." Schroeder wanted to cut the amount of money spent on the military, and once told Pentagon officials that "if they were women, they would always be pregnant because they never said 'no'." She was able to lead the way for generations of other strong women to become leaders in Washington. Women fought for their rights during the 1970s and into the succeeding decades. And while there were many setbacks, gradually many of the things that feminists wanted began to become reality.

BELL HOOKS PUTS PASSION TO PAPER

bell hooks, who was born Gloria Jean Watson to a poor family in Kentucky, is a writer, teacher, and cultural critic. She was frustrated that white female scholars were not interested in race issues and

bell hooks's book *Ain't I a Woman: Black Women and Feminism* expressed her frustration with both black and white scholars who weren't interested in black women's issues.

that black scholars were not interested in women's issues. In response, hooks wrote her first book in 1981, *Ain't I a Woman: Black Women and Feminism*. In it, she argues that race, sex, and class are at the center of black women's lives. hooks continues to write about race, capitalism, and gender and how they create systems of domination and oppression. bell hooks chose not to capitalize her pen name so that people will focus on her work and her ideas, rather than her name.

CHAPTER SEVEN

"NEVERTHELESS, SHE PERSISTED"

In the last decades of the twentieth century, and the first decades of the twenty-first, women continued to make many gains toward equality and opportunity. Many successful court cases challenged discrimination, such as assumptions that women were physically unable to perform jobs, that they must take maternity leave even if they felt capable of continuing to work, that pregnant women could not be discriminated against, and that laws should treat men and women differently.

TITLE IX

One of the most important pieces of legislation for women was Title IX (Public Law 92-318). It became law on June 23, 1972, and was meant to address extreme discrimination between men and women, especially in sports. Before Title IX was enacted, women had few opportunities to play sports, especially at the collegiate level. While there were teams, tournaments, scholarships,

By the end of the twentieth century, professional women could decide whether or not to take maternity leave and fought against pregnancy discrimination.

and funding for men's sports, there were none for women's sports. There was also a lack of facilities and equipment, as well as funds to build or buy them for female athletes. As a result, before Title IX, there were only 30,000 women nationwide participating in National Collegiate Athletic Association (NCAA) sports, compared to 170,000 men.

Title IX states: "No person in the United States shall, on the basis of sex, be excluded from participation in, be denied the benefits of, or be subjected to discrimination under any education program or activity receiving Federal financial assistance." Since almost every educational institution from kindergarten through college received some form of federal funding, Title IX applied to "state and local educational agencies including local school districts, postsecondary institutions, as well as charter schools, for-profit schools, libraries, and museums, as well as vocational rehabilitation agencies and education agencies of 50 states, the District of Columbia, and territories and possessions of the United States."

As far as sports were concerned, Title IX made sports equal in access and quality across men's and women's programs. Everything had to be equal, including locker rooms, practice and training sessions, travel funds, scholarships, equipment, and recruitment. As a result of Title IX's passage, the number of women involved in high school sports skyrocketed from 295,000 in 1972 to 2.6 million. In college sports, the numbers grew from 30,000 to 150,000.

RUTH BADER GINSBURG: HERE TO STAY

Ruth Bader Ginsburg is a Supreme Court Justice and only the second woman to be appointed to that position. She is known as an advocate for gender equality, the separation of church and state, and worker's rights. MSNBC quoted her as saying that she felt "lonely" as the only sitting female justice. "So now the perception is, yes, women are here to stay. And when I'm sometimes asked when will there be enough [women on the Supreme Court]? And I say when there are nine, people are shocked. But there'd been nine men, and nobody's ever raised a question about that." In 2009, Sonia Sotomayor joined Ginsburg as the

Sandra Day O'Connor, Sonia Sotomayor, Ruth Bader Ginsburg, and Elena Kagan (*left to right*) have all served as US Supreme Court justices.

third woman to serve on the Supreme Court, and the first Latina American.

ROE V. WADE

The 1973 Supreme Court ruling in *Roe v. Wade* gave women even more reproductive choice: the right to have an abortion to terminate pregnancies. Before the ruling, abortion was illegal in many states, unless the mother's life was endangered by the pregnancy. Women who weren't at risk sought illegal abortions, which often used questionable and dangerous methods of terminating unwanted pregnancies. The Supreme Court's ruling put an end to that and even clarified an appropriate window of opportunity for the procedure, by stating:

> *A person may choose to have an abortion until a fetus becomes viable, based on the right to privacy contained in the Due Process Clause of the Fourteenth Amendment. Viability means the ability to live outside the womb, which usually happens between 24 and 28 weeks after conception.*

With *Roe v. Wade*, women could finally access safe medical abortions legally; it was a major victory for women's reproductive rights. The ruling also became controversial, as it is considered contrary to some religious beliefs, and has become a political flashpoint between conservatives and liberals. The conflict between those who feel women have the right to choose and those who feel that unborn babies have a right to life has resulted in property damage to abortion clinics and the intimidation of female patients and abortion providers.

President Donald J. Trump's administration has announced programs that will make abortions more difficult to access. This includes allowing states to exclude proabortion organizations like Planned Parenthood from receiving federal Medicaid funding and letting health care providers refuse to perform services if their religious or moral beliefs go against such services.

SHE'S A CHEROKEE CHIEF

In 1985, Wilma Mankiller became the first woman to be elected chief of a major Native American tribe. As chief of the Cherokee Nation, she brought new energy to the tribal government and improved education, health, and housing for her tribe. She also increased nationwide membership from 68,000 to 170,000. Mankiller served until

(continued on the next page)

(continued from the previous page)

1995, and after her death in 2010, the Cherokee chief Chad Smith was quoted by the *New York Times* as saying, "We are better people and a stronger tribal nation because of her example of Cherokee leadership, statesmanship, humility, grace, determination and decisiveness."

Wilma Mankiller, chief of the Cherokee Nation, was the first woman to be elected chief of a major Native American tribe.

STILL FIGHTING

Women have made great gains in American society. These gains include equal inclusion in the military; the 2013 removal of the ban on women serving in combat positions; and the elections of Nancy Pelosi as the first female Speaker of the US House of Representatives, Condoleezza Rice as the first black female secretary of state, and Hillary Clinton's election as US senator from New York. Clinton was also later appointed secretary of state by President Barack Obama, and she subsequently campaigned for the presidency in 2016. Yet, despite these achievements, there continue to be challenges for American women to overcome.

WOMEN'S MARCH 2017

Following the election of Donald Trump as president in 2016, and his inauguration in January 2017, thousands of women all over the country participated in the Women's March. The march was organized to protest the continued hostility of powerful men to the gains made by women. This hostility was brought into stark relief by the 2016 election, in which Hillary Clinton lost as the first woman to run for president. It also raised awareness over women's reproductive rights, civil rights, and immigration. Women donned pink knit hats shaped like cat's ears, to protest a derogatory remark made by the president, and carried posters to assert the power of women, solidarity,

Ms. magazine founder Gloria Steinem speaks onstage at the rally at the Women's March on Washington on January 21, 2017, in Washington, DC.

and equal rights for all people. Feminist Gloria Steinem spoke, encouraging participants to introduce themselves to each other and decide what they were going to do tomorrow and in the days to follow, since they were never turning back.

Another incident that created a feminist rallying cry occurred on February 7, 2017, when Senator Elizabeth Warren, a Democrat from Massachusetts, was in the middle of a speech to Congress criticizing the nominee for attorney general, Senator Jeff Sessions. She was interrupted

PHENOMENAL WOMAN

African American poet, writer, and civil rights advocate Maya Angelou was the first African American woman to write a nonfiction best-seller, her memoir *I Know Why the Caged Bird Sings* in 1969. She read her poem "On the Pulse of Morning" at the inauguration of President William J. Clinton in 1993. Her book of essays, *Letters to My Daughter*, contains advice for young women about living a meaningful life. In her poem "Phenomenal Woman," she wrote:

> Pretty women wonder where my secret lies.
> I'm not cute or built to suit a fashion
> model's size
> But when I start to tell them,
> They think I'm telling lies.
> I say,
> It's in the reach of my arms
> The span of my hips,
> The stride of my step,
> The curl of my lips.
> I'm a woman
> Phenomenally.
> Phenomenal woman,
> That's me.

by Senate Majority Leader Mitch McConnell, who silenced her by invoking Senate Rule 19, which states that senators may not "directly or indirectly, by any form of words impute to another Senator or to other Senators any conduct or motive unworthy or unbecoming a Senator." When asked why he had used such a little-known rule, McConnell replied, according to the *Washington Post*: "Sen. Warren was giving a lengthy speech. She had appeared to violate the rule. She was warned. She was given an explanation. Nevertheless, she persisted."

Many women immediately protested what they saw as a man preventing a woman from speaking, and "Nevertheless, She Persisted" became a new feminist rallying cry. It has since appeared on T-shirts and other forms of media and became the theme for the March 2018 Women's History Month.

ME, TOO

In 2017, women found their voices concerning sexual harassment and abuse through the #MeToo movement. The phrase "Me Too" had first been used in 2006 as a way to help women who had suffered sexual violence. In the fall of 2017, the phrase reappeared as a hashtag on social media, encouraging women to share their own

The #MeToo movement has swept across the globe in response to the sexual harassment and abuse of women.

stories of harassment and abuse, especially in the workplace. The goal was to show the true scope of the problem and that it wasn't just limited to the emerging stories of women in the film and media industries who had experienced it for many years. Men have also suffered from harassment, contributing their own stories to the movement. #MeToo has spread worldwide in different cultural forms, starting conversations about sexual harassment and bringing awareness to the problem. *Time* magazine named "The Silence Breakers" of the movement as their 2017 Person of the Year. They said of the #MeToo movement: "The women and men who have broken their silence span all races, all income classes, all occupations and virtually all corners of the globe. They might labor in California fields, or behind the front desk at New York City's regal Plaza Hotel, or in the European Parliament. They're part of a movement that has no formal name. But now they have a voice."

For some, however, the #MeToo movement was just one step. On January 1, 2018, more than 300 women in Hollywood, California, banded together to voice more explicit goals in a published letter. This organization, TIME'S UP, "insists on safe, fair and dignified work for women of all kinds. We want women from the factory floor to the floor of the Stock Exchange to feel linked as sisters as we shift the paradigm of workplace culture."

Women's rights have made tremendous gains since the first American women struggled to be heard, to have the right to vote, and to control their own lives, opportunities, and health. As with any important change, it is a struggle that consists of forward and backward steps. As long as women are intent on making not only their lives, but also the lives of their children, fair and meaningful despite the many obstacles, nevertheless they will persist.

TIMELINE

1769 The American colonies adopt the English law that women cannot own property in their own names or keep their own earnings.

1776 Abigail Adams writes to her husband, urging him to "remember the ladies."

1848 The first women's rights convention takes place in Seneca Falls, New York.

1866 The Fourteenth Amendment is passed, officially defining citizens and voters as being male.

1890 Wyoming becomes the first state to give women the right to vote in all elections.

1916 Margaret Sanger opens a birth control clinic in Brooklyn, New York, which will eventually become Planned Parenthood.

1920 The Nineteenth Amendment is ratified, giving all women the right to vote.

1923 The first version of the Equal Rights Amendment (ERA) is introduced by Alice Paul.

1933 Frances Perkins becomes the first female US cabinet member, as secretary of labor for President Franklin D. Roosevelt.

1960 The Pill is approved for contraceptive use.

1964 Title VII of the Civil Rights Act passes, prohibiting sex discrimination in employment.

1965 The Supreme Court rules that married couples can legally use contraception.

1966 The National Organization for Women (NOW) is founded.

1972 Gloria Steinem starts *Ms.* magazine.

Title IX prohibits sex discrimination in any educational institutions that receive federal funding.

1973 The Supreme Court ruling *Roe v. Wade* makes abortion legal.

1982 The Equal Rights Amendment (ERA) fails to achieve ratification.

2013 The ban that kept women in the military from serving in combat roles is removed.

2016 Democrat Hillary Rodham Clinton becomes the first US woman to run for president from a major party. She is defeated by Republican Donald J. Trump.

2017 Thousands of women all over the United States participate in the Women's March.

The #MeToo movement is revived, protesting sexual harassment and abuse.

Three hundred women in Hollywood form TIME'S UP. an organization that says, "The clock has run out on sexual assault, harassment and inequality in the workplace. It's time to do something about it."

GLOSSARY

abolitionist A person who supported the end of the institution of slavery.

amendment An article added to the US Constitution.

anarchist One who rebels against forms of authority, including governments and ruling powers.

blitz A sudden, energetic effort to accomplish a task.

commodity A raw material or agricultural product that can be bought and sold.

contraception The purposeful use of artificial techniques or methods to prevent pregnancy.

corset A tightly fitting women's undergarment designed to shape one's figure into what was considered ideal.

crusade An organized campaign concerning a social, political, or religious issue.

forceps A large instrument with broad pincers or flat blades used to help deliver babies during the birth process.

iconic Something that is established and widely recognized, like a brand name.

invoke To appeal to or use something as an authority to support an action or argument.

iteration A new version of something.

midwife A person, usually a woman, who is trained to help women give birth.

munitions Military weapons, ammunition, equipment, and supplies.

predecessor Something that has been followed or replaced by another.

prescribed Stated as a rule or dictate that an action or procedure should be carried out.

pseudonym A false name, often used by an author to hide his or her real identity.

ratify To sign or give formal approval to something, such as a contract, document, or amendment.

satirist A person who uses humor, ridicule, or sarcasm in speech or writing, especially to expose political stupidity or personal vices.

segregation The act of separating different racial groups within communities or countries.

socialist A person who practices socialism, such as collective ownership or government ownership and administration of production and goods.

solidarity An agreement between people with a common interest.

submissive Meek or passive, obedient to someone else's authority.

subservient Less important, prepared to obey others without any question.

tariff A tax or duty paid on imported or exported goods.

FOR MORE INFORMATION

American Civil Liberties Association (ACLU)
125 Broad Street, 18th Floor
New York, NY 10004
(212) 549-2500
Website: https://www.aclu.org
Facebook and Twitter: @aclu
YouTube: aclu
The ACLU works to protect the individual rights and liberties that the US Constitution and US laws guarantee to all citizens.

Black Women's Blueprint
PO Box 24713
Brooklyn, NY 11202
(347) 533-9102
Email: info@blackwomensblueprint.org
Website: http://www.blackwomensblueprint.org
Facebook: @blackwomens.BWBNY
Twitter: @BlackWomensBP
Black Women's Blueprint is an organization dedicated to empowering black women and girls and fighting sexual violence. They hope to create a blueprint for change and to fight racial and sexual discrimination.

Canadian Women's Foundation
133 Richmond Street West, Suite 504
Toronto, ON M5H 2L3
Canada

(866) 293-4483
Email: info@canadianwomen.org
Website: https://www.canadianwomen.org
Facebook: @CanadianWomensFoundation
Twitter: @cdnwomenfdn
YouTube: CanadianWomenFdn
The Canadian Women's Foundation provides programs to work for gender equity and help women and girls move out of poverty and violence and move into leadership roles.

Center for Reproductive Rights
199 Water Street
New York, NY 10038
(917) 637-3600
Website: https://www.reproductiverights.org
Facebook: @reproductiverights
Twitter: @ReproRights
YouTube: ReproductiveRight100
The Center for Reproductive Rights works through laws to protect reproductive freedom as a fundamental human right. They feel that all governments are obligated to protect and respect this right.

Ms. Foundation for Women
12 MetroTech Center, 26th Floor
Brooklyn, NY 11201
(212) 742-2300

Email: info@ms.foundation.org
Website: https://forwomen.org
Facebook: @MsFoundationforWomen
Twitter: @msfoundation
Instagram: @msfoundation
The Ms. Foundation works on state and national levels on policies that affect women, especially minority women and low-income women. They bring attention to the challenges that these women face.

National Council of Women of Canada (NCWC)
PO Box 67099
Ottawa, ON K2A 4E4
Canada
(613) 712-4419
Email: presncwc@gmail.com
Website: http://www.ncwcanada.com
Facebook: @thencwc
The NCWC is an organization of women working together on issues that affect women, families, and communities and bringing them to the attention of their government.

FOR FURTHER READING

Atwood, Kathryn J. *Women Heroes of World War II: 26 Stories of Espionage, Sabotage, Resistance, and Rescue.* Chicago, IL: Chicago Review Press, 2013.

Blumenthal, Karen. *Hillary Rodham Clinton: A Woman Living History.* New York, NY: Feiwel & Friends, 2016.

Conkling, Winifred. *Votes for Women! American Suffragists and the Battle for the Ballot.* Chapel Hill, NC: Algonquin Young Readers, 2018.

Fabiny, Sarah. *Who Is Gloria Steinem*? New York, NY: Penguin Workshop, 2014.

Gray, Emma. *A Girl's Guide to Joining the Resistance: A Feminist Handbook on Fighting for Good.* New York, NY: William Morrow, 2018.

Hopkinson, Deborah. *What Is the Women's Rights Movement?* New York, NY: Penguin Books, 2018.

Hubbard, Ben. *Stories of Women During the Industrial Revolution: Changing Roles, Changing Lives.* Portsmouth, NH: Heinemann, 2015.

Isecke, Harriet. *Women's Suffrage: Fighting for Women's Rights.* Huntington Beach, CA: Teacher Created Materials, 2011.

Kops, Deborah. *Alice Paul and the Fight for Women's Rights: From the Vote to the Equal Rights Amendment.* Honesdale, PA: Calkins Creek Publishing, 2017.

Nardo, Don. *The Split History of the Women's Suffrage Movement: A Perspectives Flip Book.* Minneapolis, MN: Compass Point Books, 2014.

Pearson, P. O'Connell. *Fly Girls: The Daring American Women Pilots Who Helped Win WWII.* New York, NY: Simon & Schuster Books for Young Readers, 2018.

Zimet, Susan. *Roses and Radicals: The Epic Story of How American Women Won the Right to Vote.* New York, NY: Penguin Books, 2018.

BIBLIOGRAPHY

Angelou, Maya. *Letter to My Daughter.* New York, NY: Random House Trade Paperbacks, 2009.

Chittal, Nisha, and Bridget Todd. "9 powerful Ruth Bader Ginsburg quotes." MSNBC, February 15, 2016. http://www.msnbc.com/msnbc/9-powerful-ruth-bader-ginsburg-quotes.

Collins, Gail. *America's Women: 400 Years of Dolls, Drudges, Helpmates, and Heroines.* New York, NY: HarperCollins, 2003.

Collins, Gail. *When Everything Changed: The Amazing Journey of American Women from 1960 to the Present.* New York, NY: Little, Brown & Company, 2009.

Cullen-DuPont, Kathryn. "Women's Rights Movement." *The New Book of Knowledge*. Scholastic Grolier Online. Retrieved February 25, 2018. nbk.grolier.com/ncpage?tn=/encyc/article.html&id=a2031915-h&type=0ta.

Doyle, Jack. "Rosie The Riveter, 1941–1945." PopHistoryDig.com, February 28, 2009. http://www.pophistorydig.com/topics/tag/rosie-the-riveter-song.

Francis, Roberta W. "The History Behind the Equal Rights Amendment." Equal Rights Amendment: Unfinished Business for the Constitution. Retrieved March 17, 2018. http://www.equalrightsamendment.org/history.htm.

Friedan, Betty. *The Feminine Mystique.* New York, NY: W. W. Norton & Company, Inc.: 1974.

History.com. "1918: President Woodrow Wilson speaks in favor of female suffrage." Retrieved February 25, 2018. http://www.history.com/this-day-in-history/president-woodrow-wilson-speaks-in-favor-of-female-suffrage.

Jaschik, Scott. "The Evolution of American Women's Studies." *Inside Higher Ed*, March 27, 2009. https://www.insidehighered.com/news/2009/03/27/women.

"Letter from Abigail Adams to John Adams, 31 March - 5 April 1776." Adams Family Papers: An Electronic Archive. Massachusetts Historical Society. Retrieved January 19, 2018. http://www.masshist.org/digitaladams.

Library of Congress. "The Seneca Falls Convention." Digital Collections. Retrieved February 25, 2018. https://www.loc.gov/item/today-in-history/july-19.

Michals, Debra, ed. "Judith Sargent Murray." National Women's History Museum. Retrieved February 25, 2018. http://www.womenshistory.org/education-resources/biographies/judith-sargent-murray.

Moynihan, Ruth Barnes, et al, eds. *Second to None: A Documentary History of American Women*, Vol. II. Lincoln, NE: University of Nebraska Press, 1993.

Ms. magazine blog. "About: Ms. HerStory: 1971–Present." Retrieved March 17, 2018. http://

msmagazine.com/blog/about.

National Organization for Women. “Statement of Purpose: The National Organization for Women’s 1966 Statement of Purpose.” NOW.org, October 29, 1966. https://now.org/about/history/statement-of-purpose.

National Park Service. “Eleanor Roosevelt and World War II.” Eleanor Roosevelt Historic Site. Retrieved March 9, 2018. https://www.nps.gov/articles/erooseveltww2.htm.

National World War II Museum: New Orleans. “Research Starters: Women in World War II.” Retrieved March 9, 2018. https://www.nationalww2museum.org/students-teachers/student-resources/research-starters/research-starters-women-world-war-ii.

Neumann, Carynn. “Women’s Equity Action League (WEAL).” History.biz, May 7, 2015. http://www.worldhistory.biz/modern-history/83750-women-s-equity-action-league-weal.html.

Quintana, Maria L. “hooks, bell / Gloria Jean Watkins (1952–).” Blackpast.org. Retrieved March 17, 2018. http://www.blackpast.org/aah/hooks-bell-gloria-jean-watkins-1952.

“SCHROEDER, Patricia Scott, 1940–.” History, Art & Archives, U.S. House of Representatives. Retrieved March 17, 2018. http://history.house.gov/People/Listing/S

/SCHROEDER,-Patricia-Scott-(S000142).

Skelton, Chris. "Roe v. Wade, 410 U.S. 113 (1973)." Justia. Retrieved March 18, 2018. https://supreme.justia.com/cases/federal /us/410/113/case.html.

"Sojourner's Words and Music." Her Words. Sojourner Truth Memorial Committee. Retrieved February 25, 2018. http://sojournertruthmemorial.org/sojourner -truth/her-words.

Solnit, Rebecca. "Silence and powerlessness go hand in hand – women's voices must be heard." *Guardian,* March 8, 2017. https://www .theguardian.com/commentisfree/2017 /mar/08/silence-powerlessness-womens-voices -rebecca-solnit.

Sprague, Leah W. "Her Life: The Woman Behind the New Deal." Frances Perkins Center. Retrieved March 9, 2018. http://francesperkinscenter.org/life-new.

TIME'S UP. 2017. https://www.timesupnow.com /home.

US Department of Education. "Title IX and Sex Discrimination." April 2015. https://www2 .ed.gov/about/offices/list/ocr/docs/tix_dis.html.

Verhovek, Sam Howe. "Wilma Mankiller, Cherokee Chief and First Woman to Lead Major Tribe, Is Dead at 64." *New York Times*, April 6, 2010. http://www.nytimes.com/2010/04/07

/us/07mankiller.html.

Wang, Amy B. "'Nevertheless, she persisted' becomes new battle cry after McConnell silences Elizabeth Warren." *Washington Pos*t, February 8, 2017. https://www.washingtonpost.com/news/the-fix/wp/2017/02/08/nevertheless-she-persisted-becomes-new-battle-cry-after-mcconnell-silences-elizabeth-warren/?utm_term=.ac4b2ddd70dd.

Wolfe, Molly. "This Day in History: National Organization for Women was Founded." The White House: President Barack Obama, June 30, 2015. https://obamawhitehouse.archives.gov/blog/2015/06/30/day-history-national-organization-women-was-founded.

Zacharek, Stephanie, Eliana Dockerman, and Haley Sweetland Edwards. "TIME Person of the Year 2017: The Silence Breakers." *TIME* Magazine, December 18, 2017. http://time.com/time-person-of-the-year-2017-silence-breakers.

INDEX

A

abolitionist movement, 19, 21, 23, 26
abortions, 54, 55, 65, 73, 84–85
Adams, Abigail, 12–13, 14
Adams, John, 13
"Ain't I a Woman?" 26–28
Ain't I a Woman: Black Women and Feminism, 79
Allyn, Mistress, 11
American Woman Suffrage Association (AWSA), 23–24
America's Women: 400 Years of Dolls, Drudges, Helpmates, and Heroines, 10, 59
Angelou, Maya, 90
Anthony, Susan B., 22–23, 25

B

Baird v. Eisenstadt, 63
bell hooks, 77–79
Bethune, Mary McLeod, 36–37
birth control pill, 62–64
Boyer, Elizabeth, 54

C

Catt, Carrie Chapman, 29
Civil Rights Act, 52, 54, 55
civil rights movement, 36, 44, 45, 52, 53
Clinton, Hillary, 87
Coalition of Labor Union Women (CLUW), 52
Collins, Gail, 10, 17
Comstock Laws, 58–59, 61
Conroy, Catherine, 49

D

De Beauvoir, Simone, 43–44, 68

E

Equal Rights Amendment (ERA), 54, 70–74

F

Fair Labor Act, 36
Feminine Mystique, The, 47–49, 68
feminist movement, 7, 44, 56, 66, 68, 70, 75, 76, 89, 91
Fifteenth Amendment, 21, 23, 24

First Lady, role of, 34–35
Friedan, Betty, 47–50

G

gender gap, 74–76
Ginsburg, Alice E., 76
Ginsburg, Ruth Bader, 82–84
Goldman, Emma, 62
Griffiths, Martha, 54
Griswold v. Connecticut, 62–63

H

Hunt, Jane, 25
Hutchinson, Anne, 12

K

Kennedy, John F., 45
King, Coretta Scott, 53
King, Martin Luther, Jr., 52, 53

M

Mankiller, Wilma, 85–86
March for Women's Lives, 50
Marietta, Martin, 55
M'Clintock, Mary Ann, 25
#MeToo movement, 91–93
Mott, Lucretia, 25, 72
Ms. magazine, 68–70
Murray, Judith Sargent, 14–15

N

National American Woman Suffrage Association (NAWSA), 28, 29
National Association for the Advancement of Colored People (NAACP), 37
National Collegiate Athletic Association (NCAA), 81
National Organization for Women (NOW), 49–50, 54–55, 71
National Woman Suffrage Association (NWSA), 23, 24
National Women's Party (NWP), 29
National Youth Administration, 37
New Deal, 36
Nineteenth Amendment, 30

"On the Equality of the

Sexes," 15
Our Bodies, Ourselves, 65

P

Paul, Alice, 54, 70, 73
Pelosi, Nancy, 87
Perkins, Frances, 35–36,
Peterson, Esther, 46–47
Phillips, Ida, 55
Phillips, Wendell, 21
Pincus, Gregory, 63
Planned Parenthood, 61, 85
President's Commission on the Status of Women, 45

R

Rice, Condoleezza, 87
Robertson, Pat, 76
Roe v. Wade, 84–85
Roosevelt, Eleanor, 34–35, 46, 52
Roosevelt, Franklin D., 34, 35, 36, 37
Rosie the Riveter, 40–41

S

Salem witch trials, 16–17
Sanger, Margaret, 59–61, 62, 63
Schlafly, Phyllis, 73
Schroeder, Pat, 76–77
Second Sex, The, 43, 68
Smith, Abby, 22
Solnit, Rebecca, 6
Sotomayor, Sonia, 83–84
Stanton, Elizabeth Cady, 21, 22–23, 25–26, 28
Steinem, Gloria, 69, 89
Stone, Lucy, 22–23, 24, 25
Stop ERA!, 73
suffrage movement, 21, 22–23, 25, 28, 29, 68, 70
  connection with abolitionist and temperance movements, 19–21
  effect of Fifteenth Amendment on, 23–26
  winning voting rights, 29–30
Supreme Court, 55, 56, 62, 64, 82, 83, 84

T

Taft, Lydia Chapin, 11
Take Back the Night, 50
TIME'S UP, 93
Title VII, 52, 55
Title IX, 80–82
Truman, Harry S., 37
Truth, Sojourner, 26–28

V

"Vindication of the Rights of Woman, A" 6

W

Warren, Elizabeth, 89, 91
Warren, Mercy Otis, 14
"What Every Girl Should Know," 61
Wilson, Woodrow, 29
Wollstonecraft, Mary, 4–6
Women Accepted for Volunteer Emergency Service (WAVES), 39
Women Airforce Service Pilots (WASP), 39
Women's Army Corps (WAC), 38
Women's Equity Action League (WEAL), 54–55
Women's March, 87–89
Women's Rights Convention, 25, 26,
women's rights/societal roles
in Colonial America, 10–11
in the 1950s, 42–44
in the 1960s, 45–53
in the nineteenth century, 19–26
in the 1920s, 30–31
and race, 77–79
relegation to the domestic sphere, 17–18
and reproductive rights, 57–67
during World War I, 29–30
during World War II, 32–34, 37–42
women's studies, 74–76
World War I, 29
World War II, 32, 34, 35, 37–39, 40, 42, 57
Wright, Martha, 25
Wyatt, Addie L., 50, 52

ABOUT THE AUTHOR

Marcia Amidon Lusted has written numerous books and magazine articles for young readers. She is also the former editor of *AppleSeeds* magazine, part of the Cricket Media group, and continues to edit books and curriculum materials. She currently works in sustainable development for Rubicon Seven, LLC. In January 2017, she participated in the Women's March in Miami, Florida. You can learn more about her books at www.adventuresinnonfiction.com.

PHOTO CREDITS

Cover (top), pp. 27, 48 Bettmann/Getty Images; cover (bottom) Pacific Press/LightRocket/Getty Images; cover (silhouette) Kid_A /Shutterstock.com; p. 3 Rawpixel.com/Shutterstock.com; pp. 4–5 (background) Young Sam Green/EyeEm/Getty Images; p. 5 (inset) Print Collector/Hulton Fine Art Collection/Getty Images; pp. 8, 19, 32, 57, 68, 80 NASA; pp. 9, 16 © North Wind Picture Archives; p. 13 Universal History Archive/Universal Images Group/Getty Images; pp. 20, 38 Hulton Archive/Getty Images; p. 24 Carrie Chapman Catt Albums, part of the Carrie Chapman Catt Papers at Bryn Mawr College Library Special Collections Department; p. 30 Hulton Archive/Archive Photos/Getty Images; pp. 33, 72 Library of Congress Prints and Photographs Division; p. 35 Hulton Deutsch/Corbis Historical/Getty Images; p. 41 National Archive; pp. 43, 63 Keystone-France/Gamma-Keystone /Getty Images; p. 46 AFP/Getty Images; p. 51 Chicago Public Library, Vivian G. Harsh Research Collection, Rev. Addie and Rev. Claude Papers; p. 53 © AP Images; p. 58 RossHelen /Shutterstock.com; p. 60 New York Daily News Archive/Getty Images; p. 66 Barcroft Media/Getty Images; p. 69 Don Carl Steffen/Gamma-Rapho/Getty Images; p. 75 Justin Sullivan/Getty Images; pp. 78–79 The Washington Post/Getty Images; p. 81 Jose Luis Pelaez Inc/Blend Images/Getty Images; p. 83 Steve Petteway/Supreme Court of the United States; p. 86 Peter Turnley/Corbis Historical/Getty Images; pp. 88–89 Kevin Mazur /WireImage/Getty Images; p. 92 NurPhoto/Getty Images.

Design: Michael Moy; Layout: Tahara Anderson; Editor: Erin Staley; Photo Researcher: Nicole DiMella